D0544853

Ian
Carney

SUGAR BUZZ! LIVE AT BUDOKAN! ←

SUGAR
BUZZ!

Woodrow
Phoenix

Thanks,
Dan!

Contents

To all
the Louises
in the world

was

To Mum and Dad—
see, I told you all
that cartoon watching
wouldn't do me any
harm

Ian

IN THIS NEW SUGAR BUZZ SERIES WE MEET LUMBO, LUMBO AND THE FASTIDIOUS CLANCY NOTHING-FANCY. WE JOIN THEM IN THEIR EVERY-DAY LIVES - ASKING QUESTIONS, GETTING INTO MISCHIEF, HAVING FUN, FEELING APPREHENSIVE, BEING BOLD, ASKING MORE QUESTIONS.

WHY? WHAT? WHEN? WHO?

THE KEEP-KIDS-SAFE-ASSEMBLY WELCOMES TAKING CARE OF LUMBO AND LUMBO MOST ENTHUSIASTICALLY: 'IT INFORMS CHILDREN NOT TO ASSOCIATE WITH LOW-BROWS, JUGGINSES, DUMB-BELLS, NINNYHAM-MERS AND GIDDY-HEADS OF ANY NATURE.'

WHAT'S ICE CREAM HEADACHE? WILL I DIE OF IT?

WHAT'S THE DIFFERENCE BETWEEN MEN AND LADIES?

WHAT DOES A BEE HIVE SMELL OF? WHO'S JOEY LAWRENCE?

CAN I KEEP HIM? CAN I? BUT WHY? WHY?

SO READ ON. PREPARE TO LAUGH AND LEARN WHILST

TAKING CARE OF LUMBO & LUMBO

PERFECTO!

WELL, CLANCY, YOU LOOK AS SHARP AS AN OBSESSIVE-COMPULSIVE ARCHITECT'S DIAGRAM OF A KNIFE SHARPENER. ONLY SHARPER!

ALL READY FOR THE BIG DATE!!

WHEN I SAW HER AD IN THE PERSONALS I KNEW SHE WAS THE ONE FOR ME.

'ORIENTAL BUSINESS WOMAN SEEKS PROFESSIONAL MAN FOR THE PLEASURE OF PAYING ATTENTION TO DETAIL. CONTACT MS TSOI AT BOX 00001'

GAH! WHAT'S THIS? AN ERRANT NOSTRIL HAIR!!

A TOUCH OF SCHNOZZ-FUZZ IS ACCEPTABLE TO MAINTAIN A MASCULINE AIR - BUT I DON'T WANT MS TSOI TO THINK I'M SOME KIND OF SNOUT HIPPY!!

DING DONG!

ping!

AH! THAT'LL BE THE BABYSITTER!!

DING DONG! DING DONG!

COMING!

HELLO, MR NOTHING-FANCY.

AH, YOU MUST BE RUBY-ANNE.

THE AGENCY SPOKE MOST HIGHLY OF YOU.

3

4

RICK NIELSON IS THE SAME.

AMAZING! THE PAIR SEEM TO BE IN A KIND OF BEST BOY TRANCE. IT'S ALMOST AS IF THE EFFORT OF BEHAVING HAS SHUT THEIR MINDS DOWN.

I JUST HOPE NOTHING DISTRACTS THEM!

WE NEED DRINKS. NOW.

I'LL SUM-MON THE WAITER.

CLICK!

NO!

WHERE ARE WE? WHERE ARE WE? IS IT HEAVEN?

ARE WE DEAD? AM I A GHOST? AM I A SCARY GHOST WITH TEETH?

IS THAT DINNER I CAN SMELL? IS IT? CAN I HAVE SOME? CAN I HAVE PEAS? CAN I HAVE NUTS? CAN I HAVE PEANUTS?

CAN I HAVE PEANUTS? CAN I HAVE PEANUTS? CAN I HAVE PEANUTS? CAN I HAVE WALNUTS?

IS THIS A LADY? AN ADULT LADY? IS SHE WEARING A BASQUE? IS SHE PRE-MENSTRUAL?

IS IT THE QUEEN? DOES SHE HAVE WALNUTS IN HER PURSE? IS IT THE QUEEN?

DO YOU LOV RUSS THE BARBER? DOES HE CU YOUR HAIR TOO? DOES HE USE A TUREEN?

6

Valenteen in BAD HAIR DAY!

WORDS: IAN CARNEY

PICTURES: WOODROW PHOENIX

WHAT'S THIS?

VALENTEEN, THE CAVALIERE SERVENTE OF THE SUPER-HERO WORLD, FACING DEFEAT AT THE FOLLICLES OF AN ARMY OF EVIL HAIR?!

HOW COULD SUCH AN UNTHINKABLE THING COME TO PASS?

DUNCAN HEADED OFF TO SUMMON THE AMOROSO OF ACTION, STOPPING ALONG THE WAY FOR A QUICK...

≤sniff sniff!≥

Mmmm, MALE SCHNAUZER. THREE YEARS OLD. MODERATE TEMPERAMENT.

OH MY SCUT AND WHISKERS - THIS LOOKS LIKE A JOB FOR THAT BONNY BOY *VALENTEEN!*

I'LL JUST ALLOW MYSELF ONE LITTLE LICK...OH, MY! HE HAD *DOGGO* FOR TEA LAST NIGHT!

AHH, HERE IT IS. THE UNLOVED COMA WARD.

AND HERE'S UNLOVED COMA BOY *DICKIE TUMMY.*

NOW ALL I HAVE TO DO TO SUMMON VALENTEEN IS GIVE DICKIE A *GREAT BIG KISS!*

SMOOCH!♥

BUff!

LOOKS LIKE THE WORLD ONCE AGAIN NEEDS THE MASSIVE LOVE POWERS OF *VALENTEEN!*

THE DARTS ARE HAVING NO EFFECT!

COME AND HAVE A GO IF YOU THINK YOU'RE HARD ENOUGH!

GRRRRRR

OF COURSE - I SHOULD HAVE KNOWN! HAIR IS LIKE FLAKY BACK SKIN AND TOENAILS - IT CAN EXPERIENCE ENVY, REGRET AND THE OVERWHELMING SENSE OF LOSS...

DON'T LOOK NOW, DOGGY PAL, BUT THE ENEMY HAS JUST UNLEASHED ITS *HAIR FORCE!*

BUT *NEVER* LOVE. YOUR POWER COULD *NEVER* HAVE ANY EFFECT!

THUDD!

OW!

WHICH BRINGS US UP TO DATE!

HOW ARE WE GOING TO ESCAPE FROM THESE TERRIBLE TRESSES?

WE DON'T, MY LOVELY FRIEND. LET'S JUST ACCEPT OUR IMMINENT DEMISE.

WHAT?

AND IN RETURN FOR OUR SUBMISSION, I'M SURE OUR EXECUTIONERS WILL GRANT US ONE FINAL REQUEST.

WHAT'S THAT?

THAT'S FAIR ENOUGH. BLONDES DO HAVE MORE FUN.

OH YEAH, LIKE THERE *ISN'T* A MEDIA-FUELLED BLONDE BIAS.

THAT WE'RE KILLED BY A BLONDE.

US REDHEADS ARE SICK OF BEING THIRD CLASS CITIZENS!

AN INTER-HAIR CIVIL WAR BREAKS OUT!

BLONDE IS BEST!!

BETTER DEAD THAN RED!!

THINGS AREN'T ALWAYS BLACK OR WHITE!!

GREAT PLAN, VALENTEEN.

BUT ISN'T THERE A CHANCE THAT PEOPLE COULD GET INJURED IN THE HAIR HOSTILITIES?

NOPE. JUST LISTEN AS I USE MY BEWITCHING LOUDHAILER VOICE...

❤ HAIR OF THE WORLD!! ❤ ONLY TWO MINUTES REMAIN OF THE BAD HAIR DAY! UNLESS YOU FIND A HUMAN PATE AND BED DOWN, YOU WILL SHRIVEL UP AND DIE!

He's got a *LOVELY* bewitching loudhailer voice!

QUICK! FIND A HEAD!

THIS WAY!

THIS ONE'S MINE!

I SAW HIM FIRST!

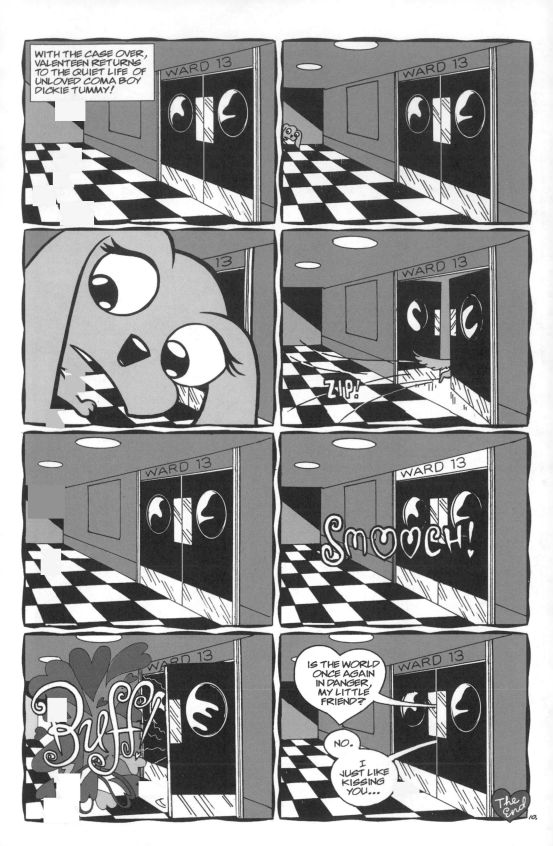

MISTER eXtra THE SUPER EVOLVED MAN

WORDS
IAN CARNEY
PICTURES
WOODROW
PHOENIX

MISTER EXTRA'S RADIANT MIND SENSES THE INEVITABLE DANGER IN THE MOST COMMONPLACE OF SITUATIONS...

STOP OLD MAN!

THE INNOCENT CONSUMPTION OF A BUTTERFLY CAKE ON THE AMERICAN SEAFRONT CAN LEAD TO A TSUNAMI OF FLAN EATING IN TOKYO!!

HALT, SEMI-ATTRACTIVE FEMALE WITH A PASSING RESEMBLANCE TO ERIK ESTRADA!!

PLAYING YOUR WHITE ZOMBIE ALBUMS BACKWARDS COULD BRING ABOUT A DISASTER OF BIBLICAL PROPORTIONS!

...NAM LIVED NAM LIVED... IIGNILLAC...

SMALL BOY!

DON'T TRY ON YOUR MOTHER'S SHOES WHILST WATCHING GLADIATOR MOVIES!

WHY - WILL IT CREATE RUCTIONS ON A COSMIC LEVEL?

NO - IT'S JUST NOT RIGHT!!

URBANE GORILLA, THE HEPPEST SWINGER IN THE WHOLE BURG, HEADS OFF TO YET ANOTHER WILD PARTY!

SO MANY COCKTAILS, SO LITTLE TIME, SO MANY WOMEN AND THEY'RE MINE ALL MINE!!

ANIMAL EXPERIMENTATION LAB

VRRRRM!

Carney-Phoenix's

Urbane GORILLA

WORDS
IAN CARNEY

PICTURES
WOODROW PHOENIX

BACK AT THE ANIMAL EXPERIMENTATION LAB, PROFESSOR POOKAH FINDS THE APE MISSING...

DRAT IT! THIS AFTERNOON I WANTED TO APPLY ELECTRICAL STIMULI TO HIS EXPOSED FRONTAL LOBES!

HEH HEH! WHAT LUCK! THE DARN MONKEY HAS LEFT HIS PSION ORGANISER BEHIND!

I CAN FIND OUT WHERE HE'S HEADING AND DRAG HIS FLEA-BITTEN HIDE BACK HERE FOR SOME VIVISECTION!

SHORTLY, AT THE OPENING OF THE CITY'S SWISH NEW ART GALLERY...

LOOK AT HIM — WHOOPING IT UP WITH THOSE WOW-MOMMAS!!

I'LL SOON KNOCK THAT SWING FROM HIS STEP.

BUT...

I'M SORRY, POOKAH - ONLY THE BEAUTIFUL AND THE STYLISH ARE INVITED TO THIS PARTY AND AS YOU'RE NEITHER...

WHAT??!!

THIS IS *PREPOSTEROUS!* I'M A RESPECTED *VIVISECTIONIST!!*

NUMBER 57 IN *ANIMAL UNDER THE BLADE QUARTERLY'S* TOP HUNDRED POWER PLAYERS...

IT'S ONE THING *BEING* AN ACADEMIC AND IT'S ANOTHER *DRESSING* LIKE ONE, DAR-LING!

HA HA HA

HA HA HA HA

BAH!

I'LL TEACH URBANE GORILLA A LESSON...

...BY *BEATING* HIM AT HIS OWN GAME!

HA HA HA HA

THE FOLLOWING EVENING, THE RICH AND HIP GATHER TOGETHER FOR THE NEXT EVENT ON THEIR SOCIAL CALENDAR...

TREMELO-CONSCIOUSNESS!

...AND I'D LIKE TO THANK YOU ALL FOR ATTENDING THE LAUNCH OF MY LITTLE RELIGION--

NOW YOU'RE PROBABLY WONDERING HOW SPIRITUAL ENLIGHTENMENT IS ACHIEVED IN OUR ORDER, AND THE ANSWER IS SIMPLE...

JUST IMAGINE A *HUGE WHAMMY BAR* ABOVE YOUR HEAD...

THINK PURE THOUGHTS...

...THEN PRESS DOWN HARD ON YOUR TREMELO ARM TO ACHIEVE A DISTORTED AND OSCILLATING PSYCHE!

BLANG!

GLAPPA CLAPPA CLAPPA CLAPP

HEY! WHO'S THAT GUY WITH THE FLIP-TOP COOL?

BEATS ME, BUT ISN'T HE THE DREAMIEST?!! *SO* DEBONAIR!!

POOKAH, WHAT ARE *YOU* DOING AT THIS PARTY?

A PARTY IS LIKE AN OLD FRIEND...UH...BEST LEFT TO STAND BEFORE CONSUMING!!

2

The Livin' END!

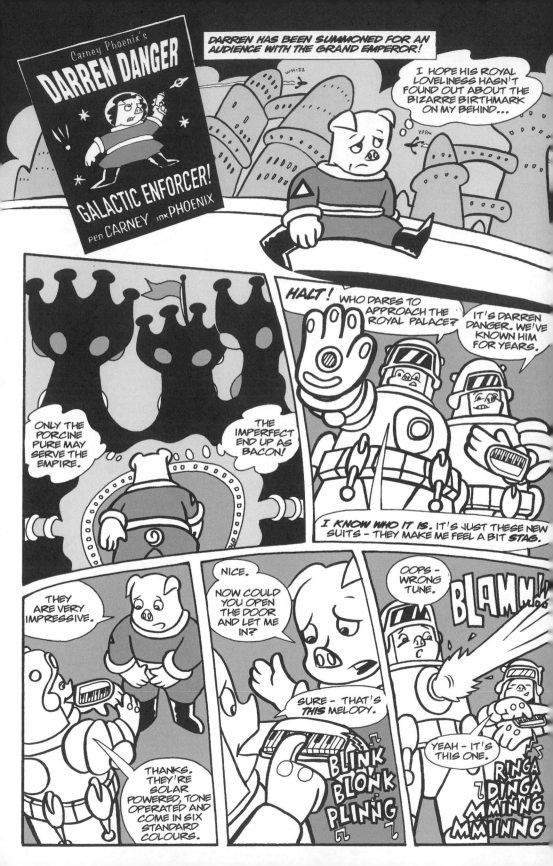

IT APPEARS TO BE A FEATHER WITH TWO FACIAL HAIRS GROWING OUT OF IT!

JUST A MINUTE — *WHAT'S* THIS?

I'LL RUN IT THROUGH MY ONPANT COMPUTER AND SEE WHAT SUSPECTS IT THROWS UP!

BEEP

THE GOATEED KITTIWAKE? NO. HE'S CURRENTLY IN JAIL. PUT HIM THERE MYSELF!

THE TOUPEED TIT? NAH. HE WAS KILLED LAST YEAR IN A MOUTHWASH/HEAVY MACHINERY INCIDENT.

THE AFFROED IBIS? 'FRAID NOT — HE SUFFERS FROM A TERRIBLE PANTS ALLERGY.

THE BEARDED SWAN? LOOKS LIKE HE'S OUR PRIME SUSPECT. BUT WHAT'S HIS MOTIVE FOR THIS TERRIBLE CRIME?

PANTSOMETER 42

THE BLOW CAUSES MAJOR INTERNAL SETTLEMENT IN CHIPSKY.

CENTRALISED AROUND HER GUT-LOCATED FILTH POUCH (STREET NAME: BOWEL)

CAPILLACEOUS TRIBUTARIES OF EFFLUVIUM RUN FROM HER BODY.

CONVERGING IN A MIGHTY RIVER OF FILTH.

IT IS A REAL ESTATE AGENT'S GREATEST NIGHTMARE: HOT AND COLD RUNNING POOP.

SHE SUBSEQUENTLY DIES.

Oooo. I'M BACK AT DEVIL'S HILLOCK.

EXCEPT THIS TIME IT'S WITHOUT YOUR CORPOREAL FRAME!

YOU LIED TO ME! THAT HOME PERM HAD NO POWER!

OF COURSE I LIED. I'M SATAN, AND NOW I'M GOING TO REINCARNATE YOUR SOUL ONTO ITS NEXT CYCLE.

EEK EEK! I'VE COME BACK AS A MOUSE!

Mmmm! THAT CHEESE SMELLS GOOD!

EEK EEK! I'LL JUST HAVE A LITTLE BI--

SLAMMM!

EEK EEK! I'M STILL ALIVE! STILL CONSCIOUS! BUT HOW? WHERE AM I?

NO! IT CAN'T BE!

NOOOOOOOOOOOO!!!

End!

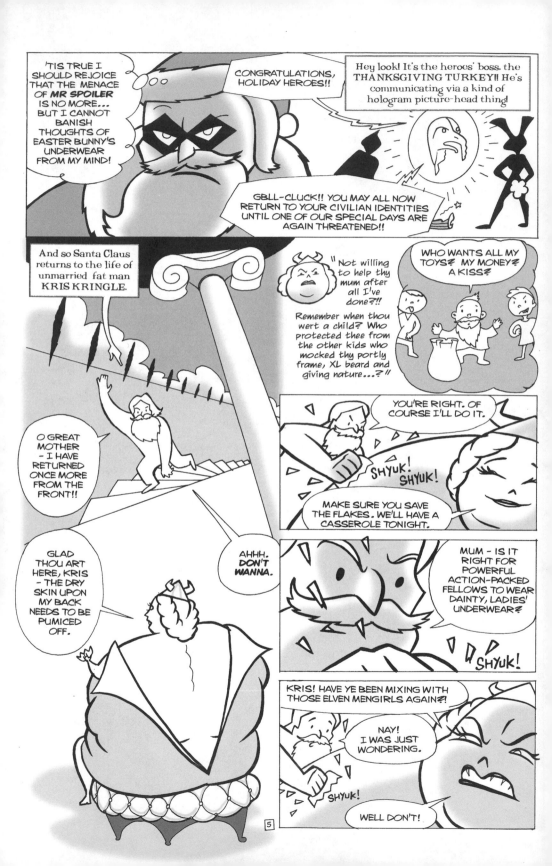

The Easter Bunny becomes a nameless rabbit and returns to her nameless burrow.

MY BUSY SUPER-HERO LIFESTYLE MEANS I DON'T GET TIME TO PROCREATE LIKE MY NAMELESS SISTER.

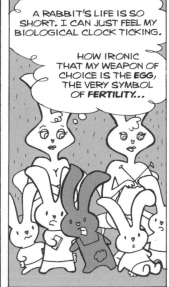

A RABBIT'S LIFE IS SO SHORT. I CAN JUST FEEL MY BIOLOGICAL CLOCK TICKING.

HOW IRONIC THAT MY WEAPON OF CHOICE IS THE *EGG*, THE VERY SYMBOL OF *FERTILITY*...

I CAN'T EXPRESS MY FEELINGS TO MY FELLOW HEROES!

HA! THEY DON'T EVEN REALISE I'M A *LADY*!

Meanwhile, HALLOWEENIE quick-changes into used dog salesman SAMUEL HAIN for a date with his girlfriend JANE GIRLFRIEND.

S-S-SORRY I'M LATE, JANE. I WAS COMING OUT OF MY APARTMENT AND GOT SCARED BY..UH..SOME STRING.

YOU'RE SUCH A SCAREDY-CAT, SAM! WHY CAN'T YOU BE FEARLESS LIKE THAT HERO HALLOWEENIE?

SO..WHAT HAVE YOU BOUGHT ME FOR CHRISTMAS?

OH...DEAR.. ..UHM

OH YES! I'VE GOT A REAL *TREAT* FOR YOU IN THIS BAG.

HOPE IT'S A RING. I *LONG* TO BE MRS JANE HAIN.

H-H-HAPPY CHRISTMAS!!!

A BIG MONSTER EYEBALL WITH HAIR GROWING OUT THE TOP?! AAAAARRGHH!!!

D-D-DARN - A *TRICK*!

6

Hey, let's keep those super-heroes' private lives private and go somewhere else.

WHERE? Helsinki, France (twinned with Helsinki, Belgium).

WHEN? 31st December.

AND THE OCCASION? the annual general meeting of the International Calendar Consortium.

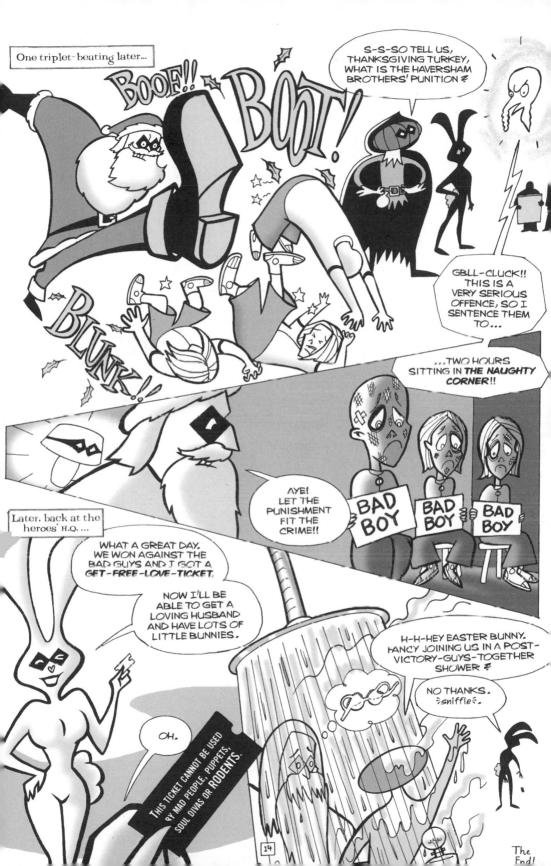

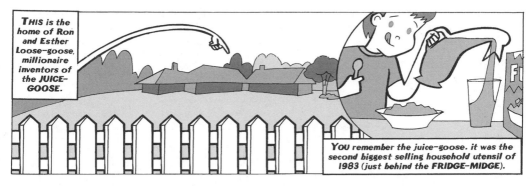

THIS is the home of Ron and Esther Loose-goose, millionaire inventors of the JUICE-GOOSE.

YOU remember the juice-goose. it was the second biggest selling household utensil of 1983 (just behind the FRIDGE-MIDGE).

This is inside the house... Shush. Let's hear what they're saying.

OH, RON. WE'RE RICH BEYOND OUR DREAMS. WE'VE GOT TWELVE BATHS AND YOUR PARENTS HAVE PEARL-INLAID HIP REPLACEMENTS... BUT STILL I'M NOT HAPPY.

I CAN NEVER BE HAPPY UNTIL WE HAVE CHILDREN.

BUT I CAN'T CONCEIVE DUE TO MY CURSED ARID WOMB.

MY MOTHER DIED OF CHAPPED LIPS WHEN I WAS YOUNG SO I NEVER REALLY KNEW HER LOVE.

ALL I HAVE TO REMIND ME OF HER IS THIS PHOTO. SHE'S SMILING ON IT. AND STANDING NEXT TO A BARGE.

DON'T LET IT GET TO YOU, ESTHER. KIDS AREN'T ALL THEY'RE CRACKED UP TO BE.

I'VE HEARD THEY'RE QUITE IMMATURE...

"AND THEY DON'T DRIVE! I'VE SEEN THEM IN THE PARK ON TINY BICYCLES WITH THESE KIND OF STABILISING ATTACHMENTS AFFIXED TO THE SIDE. RIDICULOUS!! WE DON'T WANT THAT KIND OF NONSENSE IN OUR HOUSE!!"

BUT I DO!!! YOU'VE GOT SOMETHING IN YOUR LIFE!! YOUR COLLECTION OF POLYNESIAN ORNAMENTED CRAB SHELLS KEEPS YOU HAPPY!!

WHAT HAVE I GOT?!!!

I HAVE SO MUCH LOVE TO GIVE.

YOU COULD... I MEAN, **WE** COULD ALWAYS ADOPT...

OH RON – YOU DON'T KNOW WHAT THIS MEANS TO ME.

I'LL MAKE SURE THE CHILD IS WELL BEHAVED. I'LL KEEP IT ON A LEASH AND NO GLEE OR HILARITY WILL BE ALLOWED INDOORS.

HELLO⸮ IS THAT THE **PIN-DOWN ADOPTION AGENCY⸮** GOOD. I'D LIKE TO ADOPT A CHILD.

PREFERENCES⸮ NO. NO PREFERENCES. AS LONG AS IT'S HEALTHY.

TWINS⸮ YES, WE WOULD CONSIDER TWINS. THEY'D KEEP EACH OTHER COMPANY IF WE WERE, SAY... RENDERING THE OUTHOUSE.

YOU'LL BE RIGHT OVER⸮ OKAY. SEE YOU LATER.

knock knock!

3

6

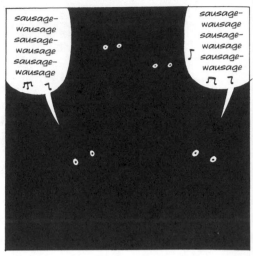

The End!!!

The SugarBuzz corporation in conjunction with Slave Labor Graphics proudly presents...

HORSE EAT DOG!

carney
words, organ, piano,
celeste, mellotron,
harpsichord,
oberheim polyphonic,
mini-moog, rice
and paper wife.

phoenix
pictures, drums,
bell-tree, tympani,
chain-driven gong,
crotales, marimba,
wind chimes, spoons
and finicky dancing.

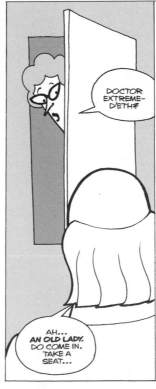

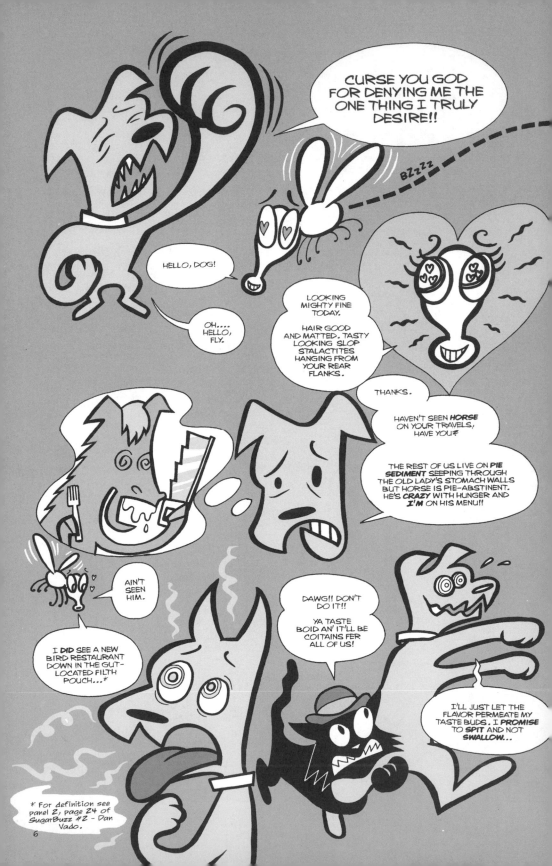

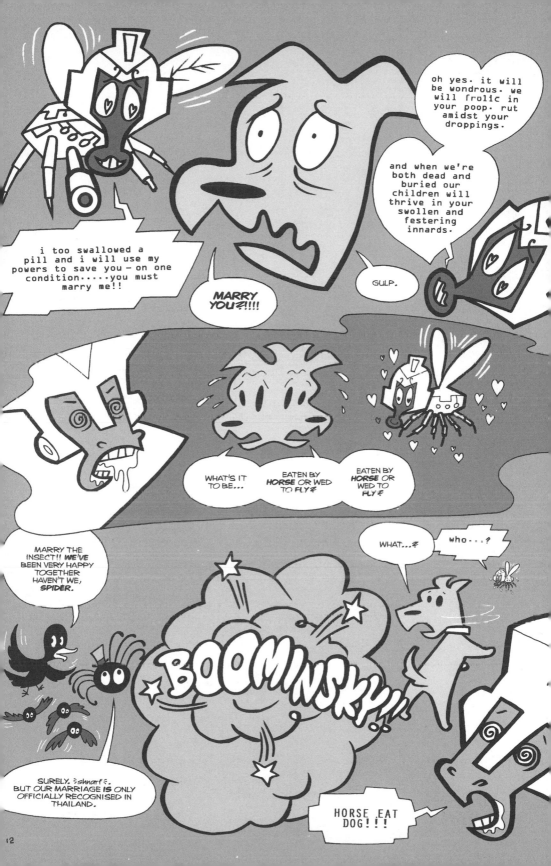

Please note: Pie Pie™ has withdrawn its sponsorship from the Haemophiliac Olympics following an unfortunate incident at the Javelin event.

Really...The End!!

Born of an illicit Man/Lamprey relationship! Blessed with the powers of the denizens of the deep! Nice costume! Has a verruca on her left foot! Hates the color brown! Has never eaten spam fritters! Let's say 'Hello Lovely Lady' to...

17

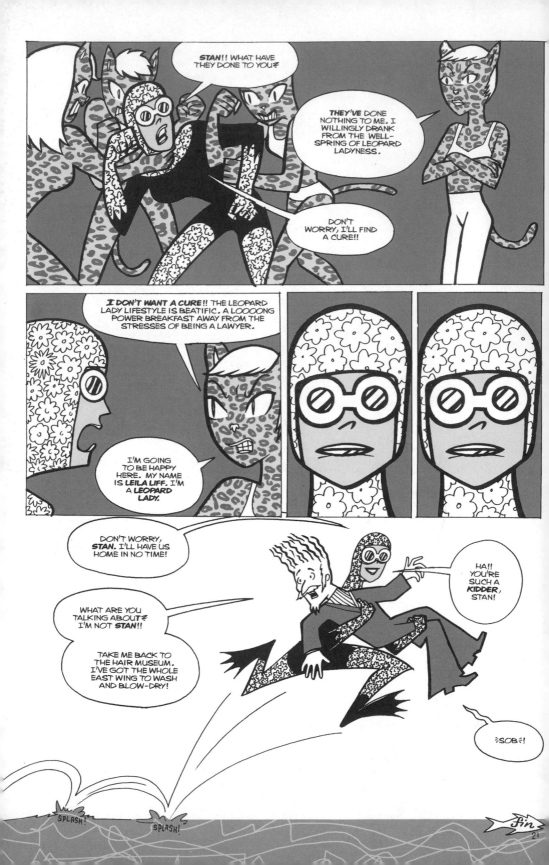

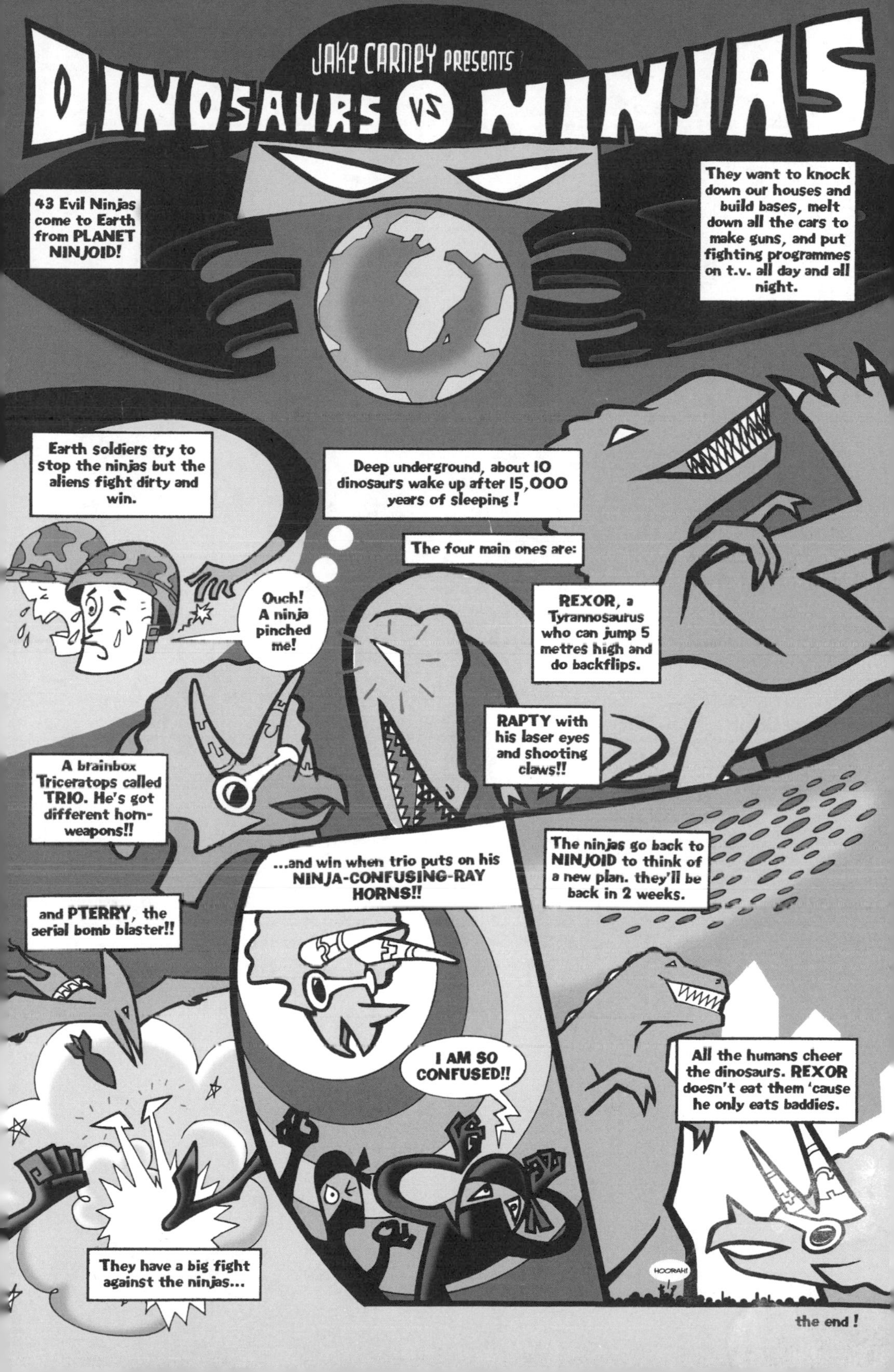
JAKE CARNEY presents
DINOSAURS VS NINJAS
43 Evil Ninjas come to Earth from PLANET NINJOID!
They want to knock down our houses and build bases, melt down all the cars to make guns, and put fighting programmes on t.v. all day and all night.
Earth soldiers try to stop the ninjas but the aliens fight dirty and win.
Ouch! A ninja pinched me!
Deep underground, about 10 dinosaurs wake up after 15,000 years of sleeping !
The four main ones are:
REXOR, a Tyrannosaurus who can jump 5 metres high and do backflips.
RAPTY with his laser eyes and shooting claws!!
A brainbox Triceratops called TRIO. He's got different horn-weapons!!
and PTERRY, the aerial bomb blaster!!
They have a big fight against the ninjas...
...and win when trio puts on his NINJA-CONFUSING-RAY HORNS!!
I AM SO CONFUSED!!
The ninjas go back to NINJOID to think of a new plan. they'll be back in 2 weeks.
All the humans cheer the dinosaurs. REXOR doesn't eat them 'cause he only eats baddies.
HOORAH!
the end !

JAKE CARNEY PRESENTS: DINOSAURS vs NINJAS

43 more Ninjas come from the planet NINJOID to conquer Earth.

They have made new Ninja machines:

The Ninja Car which can fire swords.

The Ninja Bike which can also fire swords.

The Ninja Plane which can drop a bomb that fires swords.

And the Ninja Chopper which has swords instead of propellers.

Meanwhile, the Dinosaurs are doing computers and having a workout in their underground base (1060 feet underground).

PTERRY has a quick look through the telescope and sees the Ninja machines.

I can bite through anything!!

The Dinosaurs run up the 1060 steps to the Earth's surface. Looks like there's going to be fighting! Big fighting!

The Dinosaurs throw 106 scabbards at the Ninja machines.

THE **ULTRA SPACERS** WERE MEANT TO PROTECT A HYPER-COCKTAIL WHICH VO-FARRIAN LOCUM ANARCHO-SCIENTISTS HAD BEEN FERMENTING FOR SEVEN GENERATIONS.

IT WAS SAID TO BRING ETERNAL YOUTH...

PUT THE SERUM DOWN, CHOCOLATO. **NOW!**

WHY SHOULD I? **ONE SIP** OF THIS FLUID AND I WILL BE **IMMORTAL!!**

PULL YOURSELF TOGETHER! WE'RE HERE TO **GUARD** THAT STUFF.

YOU'RE AN **ULTRA SPACER!!**

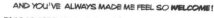

AND YOU'VE ALWAYS MADE ME FEEL SO **WELCOME!**

THIS IS GETTING BORING. I'VE REPROGRAMMED THE LOCAL SECURITY 'BOTS TO DO MY BIDDING SO – **ROBOTS: DESTROY THEM!**

WATCH THE HAIR!

SPLANG!

I'M WARNING YOU, WITH A PIECE OF CHEWING GUM, A LENGTH OF COPPER WIRE AND UNLIMITED FUNDING ONE COULD CREATE A WEAPON WHICH WOULD IMMOLATE YOUR...

SELF DESTRUCT MECHANISM ENGAGED.

SELF DESTRUCT?

BADDA BOOM!!

3

♫: CONSTANT BASS DRONE UNDERCUT BY 80S STYLE SYNTH STABS

...I'M *DENNIS MORRETTA*. FROM B.O.P. * CENTRAL COMMAND.

IT'S A GREAT PRIVILEGE TO MEET YOU, MS DA SILVA...

DO YOU HAVE THE PIXELWORK?

* B.O.P. - BUNCH OF PLANETS - THE ULTRA SPACE CONFEDERATION OF WORLDS.

I THINK YOU'LL FIND IT ALL IN ORDER...

YOU'VE NEGLECTED TO COMPLETE FORM GGG447X. I'LL EXPECT IT ON MY DESK BY 09.00 TOMORROW MORNING.

UH..RIGHT.

I KNOW THIS MIGHT BE DIFFICULT FOR YOU; ME COMING HERE TO ASSESS YOUR WHOLE *LIFE* WITH A VIEW TO *CLOSING IT DOWN.*

IT'S NOT A PROBLEM FOR *ME*, MR MORRETTA.

YOU MAY REMEMBER THAT WHEN I WAS AN ACTIVE ULTRA SPACER MY SPECIALITY ABILITY WAS MY *ADMINISTRATIVE PROWESS...*

I'M ALL FOR CUTTING AWAY COSTLY DEAD WOOD.

I'M JUST SURPRISED CENTRAL COMMAND HANDED THE PRUNING SHEARS TO ONE SO *YOUNG.*

YOU'RE CERTAINLY JUST AS TOUGH AS YOU EVER WERE. I SUPPOSE YOU ULTRA SPACERS ARE BUILT TO LAST.

dutch castro: deceased

lester pate: inactive

chocolato: evil fella

NOT ALL OF US. YOU'VE SEEN THE DISCS.

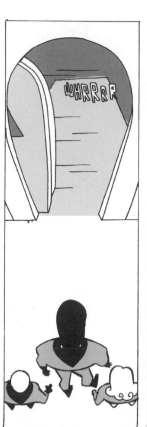

...LESTER'S **STILL** MY HUSBAND. I THINK I STILL LOVE HIM.

I DON'T KNOW. WE LIVE TOO LONG NOWADAYS, TOOTS. LOVE'S ONLY GOT A FORTY YEAR SHELF LIFE.

WHEN HE HAD A BODY HE DIDN'T SEEM THAT INTERESTED IN.. y'know.. THE JIGGY STUFF. NOW THAT'S **ALL** HE THINKS ABOUT.

HE'S A MAN. WE DON'T LIVE AS LONG AS YOU BABES.

WE HAVE TO FIT A LIFETIME'S WORTH OF THINKING ABOUT THE JIGGY STUFF INTO A SHORTER SPACE OF TIME.

LESTER FITS AN AVERAGE PERSON'S LIFETIME OF THINKING ABOUT THE JIGGY STUFF INTO AN AFTERNOON.

NO, WAIT – THAT'S **YOU.**

HEH, I DON'T **THINK** ABOUT IT. JUST **DO** IT.

I'VE PUNTED MORE BARGE THAN YOU'VE HAD **HOT DINNERS!**

OKAY. SO I'M A LITTLE **HIPPIER** THAN I USED TO BE...

I DIDN'T MEAN..hmmm. SORRY.

...HAVE YOU EVER SEEN A **CAT,** ESTHER?

IS THAT THE THING YOU USED TO GET MILK FROM. **NO** – THAT'S A **HORSE.**

ACTUALLY, THAT'S A **COW...**

A CAT WAS A SMALL DOMESTIC ANIMAL.

THEY WERE **EVERYWHERE** UNTIL IT WAS DISCOVERED THAT THE HAIR OF THE CAT WAS AN EFFECTIVE HANGOVER CURE. THE SPECIES DIED OUT IN A DECADE.

MY OLD MAN SAW A STUFFED GINGER TOM IN A MUSEUM IN BELGRADE.

SAID IT WAS THE MOST BEAUTIFUL THING HE'D EVER SEEN. USED TO THINK ABOUT IT EVERY TIME HE MADE LOVE.

GUM? DIET GUM...

THANKS.

I'VE NEVER HEARD YOU MENTION YOUR FATHER BEFORE.

yeah. I WAS ALWAYS A BIG DISAPPOINTMENT TO HIM.

I REMEMBER THIS ONE PARTICULAR DAY. THE OLD MAN SAID HE WAS GOING TO BUY ME A MOVIE DISC AND I JUST COULDN'T DECIDE WHICH ONE.

HE WAS PRESSING ME TO CHOOSE **GLADIATORS VS VIKINGS : TO THE DEATH!**, BUT I HAD MY EYE ON **DANCE MAGIC WITH BARBARA TIPPY TOES**.

ANYHOWS, I PLUMPED FOR BARBARA TIPPY TOES...**GREAT** LEGS...THE OLD MAN DIDN'T SAY ANYTHING BUT I KNEW I'D KINDA LET HIM DOWN.

WE WERE NEVER THAT CLOSE AFTER THAT.

DID YOU MAKE UP BEFORE HE DIED?

OH HE'S NOT DEAD. HE'S IN A HOME DOWN ON THE OUT-TO-PASTURE PLANET.

19

ULTRA SPACE HAS TEN HOURS BEFORE IT IS TUGGED OUT OF EXISTENCE.

THE ULTRA SPACESHIP IS FUELLED AND READY. YOU LEAVE *NOW*.

YOU CAN *COUNT* ON US, BLANCHE (LITTLE ADMINISTRATIVE JOKE THERE).

WE EASILY DEFEATED THE PUPPET KING AND WE'LL SAVE THE DAY TODAY!

WYAK WYAK!

NOW WHERE WAS THE PROBLEM AGAIN?

≷cough cough!≷

HAVE I GOT TIME TO ZIP HOME AND GET MY PUZZLE BOOK?

TEN HOURS...

I'M SORRY, SIR, ALL FLIGHTS OUT OF ULTRA SPACE ARE BOOKED UP FROM NOW UNTIL THE END OF TIME. WHICH IS ABOUT NINE HOURS AWAY.

PLEASE...I'VE GOT TO GET BACK TO BARTH. MY WIFE'S THERE..

THIS PIE PIE PIE™ *IS* DELICIOUS.

NYAH NYAH NYAH NYAH NYAH! I'M DESTROYING ULTRA SPACE! NYAH NYAH NYAH NYAH NYAH!

BUT WHY, DEARIE?

YOU USED TO BE AN ULTRA SPACER!!

OH YEAH – I'M SUPPOSED TO PRESS THIS!

BZZT!

AH...*ULTRA SPACERS!*

I'M RECORDING THIS BECAUSE I REALISE I WON'T BE MATURE ENOUGH TO GLOAT PROPERLY BY THE TIME YOU SEE IT.

YES, THE UNIVERSE IS ENDING. YES, I'M RESPONSIBLE.

WHAT DID YOU SAY, ADELE – "BUT WHY, DEARIE?"

DIDN'T SAY A THING, **DEARIE.**

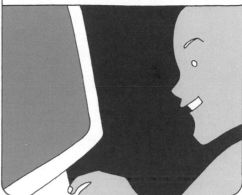

THE VO-FARRIAN CONCOCTION WORKED. I NEVER AGED A DAY. I WAS BORED WITH THE WHOLE HERO/VILLAIN THING SO I TRIED SOMETHING NEW. WROTE THE **LADY DERBYSHIRE** SERIES OF HISTORICAL ROMANCES UNDER THE PEN NAME **LUCY EVIL.**

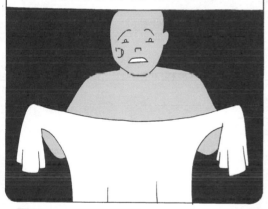

LIFE WAS PEACHY UNTIL I NOTICED I WAS SHRINKING. A COUPLE OF TESTS CONFIRMED THAT I WAS ACTUALLY GETTING **YOUNGER**, PROBABLY BECAUSE I TOOK MORE THAN A **SIP** OF THE ANTI-AGEING SERUM.

TERRIFYINGLY, THE EFFECT WAS CUMULATIVE. I WAS HURTLING TOWARDS MY BIRTH AT A RATE OF A YEAR EVERY TWO WEEKS.

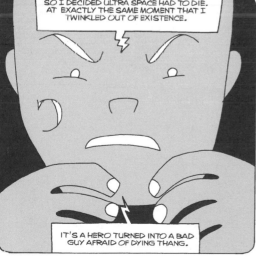

SO I DECIDED ULTRA SPACE HAD TO DIE. AT EXACTLY THE SAME MOMENT THAT I TWINKLED OUT OF EXISTENCE.

IT'S A HERO TURNED INTO A BAD GUY AFRAID OF DYING THANG.

WHICH IS WHERE **THIS** DEVICE CAME INTO PLAY...

...THE ELSON ARTEFACT, AN ANCIENT RELIC WHOSE EXISTENCE HAS MYSTIFIED MAN FOR A HUNDRED YEARS.

ONLY *MY* INTELLECT COULD DETERMINE ITS PURPOSE — A METAPHYSICAL UBER-MACHINE WHICH, IN LAYMAN'S TERMS, COULD BE DESCRIBED AS *GOD'S CAR VAC.*

I REALISED THAT WORKING, THIS THING COULD SUCK UP THE COOKIE CRUMBS OF REALITY — EVENTUALLY DRAWING ITSELF INWARDS AND CREATING A BLACK HOLE WHERE ONCE SPRAWLED ULTRA SPACE.

SO I HAD A DABBLE AT GENOCIDE AND STOLE THE DEVICE. NEXT PROBLEM WAS HOW TO POWER THE THING.

pie pie pie™

TA-DA! I CREATED PIE PIE PIE™ FOR THE PURPOSE.

GASP!

MMMMM. DELICIOUS.

EACH WRAPPER HAS A QUANTUM CONVERSION BARCODE ON THE WRAPPER. EVERY TIME ONE OF THEM IS SCANNED THE DATA IS CONVERTED INTO ENERGY FRAGMENTS WHICH THE MACHINE ABSORBS.

BILLIONS OF PIES SOLD. MACHINE FULLY POWERED. NO OFF SWITCH. UNIVERSE POPS. BYE BYE.

BET YOU WISH YOU'D BEEN A BIT NICER TO ME NOW, EARL!

we could...ask everyone in ultra space to...TAKE THE PIE PIE PIES™ BACK.... return them to the shops...

YES! THAT'S IT! THAT'S THE PLAN!!

COMMUNICATIONS ARE DOWN...COULD USE MY TELEPATHIC POWERS TO PERSUADE THE PUBLIC... GONNA NEED A POWER BOOST FOR THAT....MAYBE EXCESS ENERGY FROM THE MACHINE?

UH... I COULD PUNCH SOMETHING OR MAKE LOVE TO SOMEONE?

COULD BE RISKY BUT WHAT HAVE WE GOT TO LOSE? LET'S GO FOR IT...

OH DEARIE!! MAJOR POWER UP!!!

DO YOU THINK I'M STUPID? ALL OF IT..THE PUPPET KING AND THE RETURN OF CHOCOLATO.. IT'S ALL A SCAM TO MAKE THE ULTRA SPACERS LOOK GOOD!

REALLY, THE CHOCOLATO THING WASN'T..

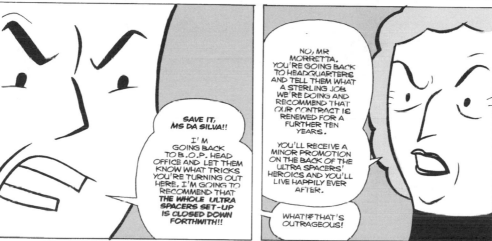

SAVE IT, MS DA SILVA!! I'M GOING BACK TO B.O.P. HEAD OFFICE AND LET THEM KNOW WHAT TRICKS YOU'RE TURNING OUT HERE. I'M GOING TO RECOMMEND THAT **THE WHOLE ULTRA SPACERS SET-UP IS CLOSED DOWN FORTHWITH!!**

NO, MR MORRETTA, YOU'RE GOING BACK TO HEADQUARTERS AND TELL THEM WHAT A STERLING JOB WE'RE DOING AND RECOMMEND THAT OUR CONTRACT IS RENEWED FOR A FURTHER TEN YEARS.

YOU'LL RECEIVE A MINOR PROMOTION ON THE BACK OF THE ULTRA SPACERS' HEROICS AND YOU'LL LIVE HAPPILY EVER AFTER.

WHAT!? THAT'S OUTRAGEOUS!

YOU HURT MY TEAM IN **ANY WAY** AND THIS VIEW-DISC OF YOUR FRANKLY STOMACH-CHURNING LOVEPLAY WITH BUNNY FERRANTI WILL BE IN **DEAR MELANIE'S** HANDS THE FOLLOWING MORNING.

♫: SLAPSTICK PARP OF A TROMBONE.

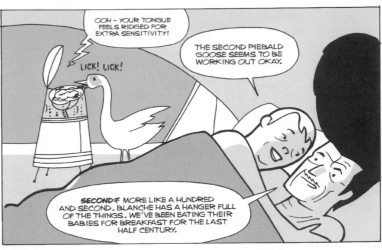

33

♪: ROUSING HALF-SPEED GUITAR ARRANGEMENT OF THE ULTRA SPACERS THEME. BY STEVIE STEVENS.

THE END!

Rebecca, meanwhile, established a mobile detective agency mainly dealing with adultery, and hauntings by maleficent goat-breathed nasties.

WELL WHERE'S IT AT, SUGAR KAT?!

I'M A **HUGE** FAN. COULD YOU SIGN MY PACK OF **SILICON CHICKEN NIPPLES?**

SURE. SAY, DO **YOU** USE THESE FOR WEANING ORPHANED POULTRY OR FOR SOME SORT OF SCAREY NAKED THERAPY THING?

BOTH!

PRESUMABLY WE CAN RULE HIM FROM THE INVESTIGATION - HE'S TOO FAT TO BE THE DOG-DEMON.

DIDN'T YOU NOTICE THE CORSET HANGING ON THE BACK OF THE DOOR? WEARING THAT HE COULD EASILY SQUEEZE INTO THE COSTUME.

UH OH!

YOU DID NOT HEED MY WARNING AND SO NOW YOU MUST FEEL THE POWER OF MY POWERFUL POWER!!!

IT'S POWERFUL!!

EEP!

YEARBOOK'S DIED OF FRIGHT AGAIN!!

LET'S JUST **GET AWAY!** WE CAN REVIVE THE CAT WHEN WE GET TO SAFETY!

YOUR TURN TO KISS HIM!

MY NAME IS *JUDY.*

THE SPACE DOG!! AND YOU CAN *TALK*!!

AFTER THE SPACE BASE CLOSED DOWN I REALLY THOUGHT THE WORLD WAS MY OYSTER.

I WENT TO COLLEGE AND GOT A DIPLOMA IN HOME ECONOMICS, DEVELOPED AN INTEREST IN WINE MAKING...

INDEED, THANKS TO ALL THE SMART DRUGS THAT WERE PUMPED INTO ME...

VACANT POSITIONS

RTUAL RLFRIEND	KINDLY OLD FATHER FIGURE	DARLING BRICKLAYER	HOOVERER	TOOTH FAIRY
O SAPIENS ONLY	NO DOGS	NO DOGS	NOT DOGS	HUMANS ONLY
PARTMENT RE DETECTIVE	PRIVATE TICKLER	ECUMENICAL STUNTMAN	PRESIDENTIAL STOOGE	KING FOR A DAY
OGS ORA	POOCHES, NO	NIX 4 DOGS		BIPEDS ONLY NEED APPLY
O SP	NUCLEAR TESTER	TER MISS	LING VERT	HAMBURGER HELPER
D	NO DOGS			PAS DE CHIEN
	ZIRKUS AFFE			CHEESE STIRRER
	NO DOGS			DON'T EVEN THINK ABOUT IT, WOOFERS

BUT ONCE OUT IN THE REAL WORLD I DISCOVERED THAT DOGS WERE TENTH CLASS CITIZENS. EVEN LOWLIER THAN ALBINOS.

THIS IS A CRUEL WORLD FOR DOGS.

BAD BOY! BAD *BAD* BOY!!

I FEED YOU A DIET OF TINNED CATTLE LIPS, DEHYDRATED PORK INNARDS AND TABLE SNACKS AND NOW I'M BOTH SURPRISED AND ANGRY THAT YOU'RE PRODUCING BAD BACK-WIND ODOURS!!

RETURNING TO THE SPACE BASE I DISCOVERED THAT THE ROCKET HAD NOT BEEN DISMANTLED.

WITH A BIT OF WORK IT COULD BE REFURBISHED. I COULD TAKE ALL THE LOCAL DOGS INTO SPACE TO FIND A NEW WORLD.

IN A STRANGE TWIST OF CIRCUMSTANCE, I DISCOVERED I WAS LACTATING SMART JUICE AND SO I INCREASED THE INTELLECT OF MY FELLOW CANINES BY 109%.

NEXT STOP: THE DOG STAR!!
BOOOOM!
REBECCA!! I...
KEEP AWAY FROM ME!
I THOUGHT WE HAD NO SECRETS, BUT ALL THIS TIME YOU'VE BEEN HIDING YOUR DOG-DEMON WAYS FROM ME...

Will Kane
meets the
Carney/Phoenix.
Be afraid. Be
very afraid.

Ian Carney

Will Kane

Woodrow Phoenix

Will Kane: I thought I'd start this interview by asking you about your backgrounds since SugarBuzz! draws so much from your childhood and childhood experiences.

Ian Carney: Typical happy childhood, completely obsessed with comics and cartoons. I remember coming back from the dentist after having a tooth taken out and being mildly giddy on the gas and walking into the newsagent on Mill Lane and my Mum buying me a Spider–Man comic. I actually thought "Wow! This doesn't look like an ordinary comic." I sat at home in my bedroom staring at this comic and the colours were actually shimmering above the pages. I also couldn't get enough of cartoons — 60's Hanna-Barbera stuff. When we got our first colour TV my parents said to me, "Now you'll be able to watch all the cartoons in colour." And I replied "What are you talking about? They're in colour anyway, Daffy Duck's bill is yellow!"

Woodrow Phoenix: The first thing I saw on a colour TV was a Tom and Jerry short which was probably the best thing to see because it was so vivid ...loud...lush.

IC: My Dad liked Tom and Jerry.

WP: Dads do...it's proper drawing.

IC: Every time the opening credits rolled to 'produced by Fred Quimby' my Dad insisted on shouting "Good old Fred" for no apparent reason. It became a family ritual, a bonding thing.

Living in Britain we were cut off from a certain amount of American things.

WP: Cardboard two-man subs, Twinkies...

IC: We both used to get DC comics in the late 60's and there were those ads for the saturday morning cartoon line-ups. And we used to just look at them and go "Wow!" It was definitely a case of forbidden fruit. I'd become obsessed about cartoons like Fat Albert, Gilligans Planet... I'm sure if I'd seen

them I'd have thought they were lame, it was just the fact that they were all cartoons that we had no chance of seeing — one of them could have been the best cartoon ever. The ones I did see that made an impression were Rocket Robin Hood, New Adventures of Huck Finn, Frankenstein Jr. and the Impossibles.

WP: I didn't have that same kind of fascination with Hanna–Barbera in particular, I just liked anything animated. The things I liked the most were probably the UPA cartoons like Mr Magoo. And The Pink Panther Show. I loved the way that everything was geometric and designed.

IC: Why don't you try and get some of that in your artwork? [laughter]

It wasn't just the comics and cartoons we had over here, we had things like the Batman TV show and Bewitched and those sorts of things appealed to you as well.

WP: It's an ideal scenario, people live these wonderful lives where everything is convenient and stylish and they all live in these lovely homes and have all these possessions. But, still, there's this extra added twist, with this other nutty stuff going on. And of course Bewitched and I Dream of Jeannie were both very frustrating because, if you had a magical wife, then you'd get them to do what you wanted all the time, wouldn't you? And for some reason, these two women just happened to find the two men in the whole of America who didn't want what they had, what they had to give. And I'd just spend my afternoons watching these things being really frustrated, saying "Why, why can't you just let them do what they want?!WHY?!!"
In terms of comics I read everything. We went on holiday to the Isle of Wight and holidays are always fertile places to go looking because they're off your ordinary path, so you find unusual stuff, and I remember one day I went on a comics trawl and I found a collection of strips called 'How to play golf the Gary Player way' and it was drawn by somebody in that Stan Drake, sharp-edged, black and white style. And the drawing was fantastic. It didn't matter that I didn't know or care anything about golf, I was just completely captivated by the drawing. I was probably only about nine or ten, I used to read this thing over and over.

...I was just standing there with blood coming down my face going "COMICS!!"

But, there's also the juxtaposition between what the USA looked like to us, and what England looked like; despite what all the Beatles movies were making out England looked like, England looked a lot different to that.

WP: And that's what we were attracted to, apart from that everyone was young and dynamic and had those great houses and lovely cars.

Do you think this flavours the way you approach the American subject matter, because SugarBuzz looks like an American comic, but it's drawn by two British people who see the USA differently to the way an American would.

IC: I think we kind of do the US comic or maybe cartoon thing but we get it wrong. But in our favour. I think there's probably other people doing the same thing as us but getting it more to the template.

Because there's a few other people doing similar sorts of things to you aren't there?

IC: Obviously, it's just a baby boomer thing. I mean it is a sub-genre, but then there's thousands of comics doing Jack Kirby things. Growing up in Wallasey, a small town, I was reading all these comics and going to conventions and that. But I never actually knew any one who was into comics. At school, everyone used to mock me, they actually used to call me "Yank" for quite a while because I read American comics all the time. Even to this day, sometimes I'll be shopping in town and meet someone from school and they'll say "Hello Carney!" in a 'Hello Newman' style. They'll go "Hello Carney, still reading Spider–Man are you?!" I always tell Carole, my wife, my ambition is to write one Spider–Man story so I can say "No, actually I'm writing Spider–Man."

Like that's really going to impress them.

IC: They'll probably just beat me up won't they, like school? So I had no one to talk to about comics, and then, this was probably early eighties, I was in Liverpool at a comic shop which had loads and loads of back issues as well as porn mags and horror stuff. And I met two guys from Liverpool who were both trying to become comic artists. I just happened to start talking to them in the shop and we ended up going to the pub around the corner and just talking

about comics for five hours non-stop, it was a whole lifetime of talking about comics—

WP: Yeah, I remember those.

IC: —and I was just like "And do you remember when Gwen Stacy died?!! And what about so and so ?!! And what about Krypto?!! And what about blah blah?!!" I was talking so fast and getting so worked up that my nose just, like, POPPED and two streams of blood squirted out from each nostril and splattered all over the table and these two lads were like horrified and I was just standing there with blood coming down my face going "COMICS!!" Actually I had a notepad which I've still got to this day where I captured some of the blood on the paper and dated it. [laughter] I could probably tell you the exact date of that...

WP: ...Comics haemorrhage. [laughter]

Let's talk about when you started getting stuff published. When you made your first fledgling steps into this business we call comic.

IC: Woodrow was first.

WP: Paul Gravett had just started publishing Escape which was a magazine which aimed to do for British comics what magazines like The Comics Journal, I guess were doing for American comics. Except that it was an odd mixture of things because in some ways Escape was more an antidote to what was going on in comics at the time, because it was meant to show that we had as much or more in common with continental comics as we did with the 'States. That was kind of interesting, a combination of text features and strips. So my first strip that got seen by more than about twenty people was in Escape. It was a reprint of something I self published. And that was another style I approximated and that was based on the style of a bloke called Patrick Nagel who drew for Playboy and he drew these very, very glamourous very, very sophisticated figures...

And drew the Duran Duran Rio cover.

WP: Yeah, that's the one. It amused me to draw a comic strip that had all these sophisticated characters at dinner. One of them turns up with his new girlfriend who turns out to be a Martian who essentially looks like a big wedge of fudge, very unglamourous, and everyone's horrified. Just playing around with the idea and seeing what happens.

It's like Guess who's coming to Dinner but instead of Sidney Poitier, she's an alien. Do you think one of the reasons why British people are able to break into American markets in a slightly bigger way than continental Europeans or the Japanese is because we are sort of half way between the USA and Europe so we have sort of a European sensibility but an American sensibility as well?

WP: Well, I think, obviously because we do have that language advantage where... it's an advantage and a disadvantage because on the one hand we don't have really, to work very hard to translate things but on the other hand it's a disadvantage because North American culture is actually quite different. We think it's similar because our languages are superficially the same but when you actually go to the 'States you realise it's a foreign place, people are different there and they don't have the same kind of thoughts and ideas. There are lots of similarities but it's not the same so it's kind of a trick.

IC: Wales is a bit like that. [laughter]

WP: So in some ways the stuff coming out of France and Belgium and Germany is just as relevant to us as anything out of the USA. They just feel more remote because they need translating.

So, Carney? Early comics stuff?

IC: Well, I was a little bit comics, a little bit rock and roll. I was playing with the band semi-professionally on and off for about ten years and I just came to the stage where it's like "Wow, I'm not going to make this after all, this is not going to happen." After so many years of being...I mean, most things I approach shouting "YES! I'm going to do this, nothing's going to stop me doing this!" and I had that attitude for about ten years and then eventually, I was just like "I played a club last night, and I played that club ten years ago and

there were the same fifteen people there who were shouting: WANKER!" [laughter]
So I decided well, I'd better find something else to do and I started reading other comics, moving on from Shogun Warriors. I'd got into that early 80's comic stuff like Nexus and Cerebus and Love and Rockets and American Flagg. I'd been writing songs and writing various text pieces for various things and I just thought y'know, I'll try writing comic scripts. So I wrote a Judah the Hammer back up strip — I noticed there were varying writers, it was the first thing I sent off and two weeks later First Comics phoned and said y'know "We quite like it, can we have some more."

This was in Nexus?

IC: Yeah, this was in Nexus. So, it's like "Oh, wow they're not phoning up and shouting 'WANKER!!'" So I did some of that and y'know small press stuff and various other things but I suppose that was my... first published thing. I did six or seven of them and then some more small press stuff, stuff for Fantagraphics and Marvel UK; Power Rangers, Rugrats.

You started writing Randy the Skeleton.

IC: Randy the Skeleton, which was the first time I started to notice... Randy was so free, so abstract, and...

Just like free form jazz.

IC: It was like free form jazz. But the good thing about that was...I mean I'm always saddened by the lack of ideas in comics, there just seems to be the same ideas around. With a medium where it is so free, there's no budgets, in a lot of cases no one telling you what you can and can't do, I was just so dismayed at how few ideas there were, so one thing I enjoyed about Randy the Skeleton was...

It was just ideas.

IC: I remember an editor saying to me "The thing about Randy the Skeleton is that I always come to a panel and I think, well that story could have gone off in that direction but it didn't, it went over there. I'd have liked to have seen what happened if the story had gone there, but then I'd get to the next panel and I'd think the same thing." I thought that was good. And one of the greatest compli-

Gorillas with guns are going berserk, and they're just skating over it on the news?!!"

ments was when I showed the Randy strip to a girl I knew and she was reading through it. She obviously wasn't comics literate and she was trying to make head or tail of it and she actually looked at the caption box and said "These words in these boxes, is that you talking?" And I said "What makes you say that?" and she said "Well, it just sounds like you." and I thought "Oh, yeah, that, that's good."

Did you feel like Robin Williams in Dead Poets Society? Like an inspirational force?

IC: I felt more like Robin Williams in Mrs Doubtfire. [laughter]

WP: My first mass media thing was The Sumo Family. It was an idea I came up with on holiday in Spain with my then girlfriend Charmaine. We'd sit on the beach every day and there'd be this really hugely enormous fat bloke with a really hugely enormous fat baby in a pushchair and unfortunately his wife was quite slim so that spoiled the image slightly, but we got to calling him the sumo guy with the sumo baby then I started drawing him in my sketch book and I realised there was a strip in it. I broke down the idea and it turned into one of those Art strips where the whole point was this character was too big, too big for the strip he was in so he was very confined by the panel borders, and he was always trying to break out of them. I liked that idea and played around with it quite a lot and then, I don't know quite what happened but then it occured to me that it would be quite easy to do a whole strip based around these sort of characters.
When I started thinking about how to approach it, the idea of making it into a Flintstoney kind of strip but still keeping a lot of those absurdist, existentialist elements, I thought there must be a way to combine these two elements and I talked about it with Paul Gravett and Peter Stanbury, the editors of Escape and they thought so too. So in some ways I could credit them with quite a lot of the impetus for getting it going. Because once they expressed an interest and I think suggested a couple of ideas then I sat down and tried to do this kind of thing which looked on the surface like that kind of sitcommy cartoon but had another layer of intellectual nonsense to it. So the first one which I did for Escape has all those hallmarks on it — and the response made me think there was something there

worth pursuing. Because I'd always thought comics were not something you could make money out of, but I thought possibly a newspaper strip might be one way to do it. So, when the Independent on Sunday started up...

Which is a national newspaper over here.

WP: ...and I noticed that they didn't have any strips, I just thought "What the hell, I'll give it a go and see what happens." So I rang them up and said "You haven't got any comic strips, do you want one?" and they said "Well actually we've got something about to start right now and it's running for the next few weeks, but come and see us and we'll see what you've got." I showed them the Sumo Family and they quite liked it and they agreed to give it a trial run. So I had to produce roughs for about twenty strips so that they could see it had some longevity to it and they agreed to do it. So the first one came out and that was very exciting, looking at this full colour strip in this national newspaper. I only did it for about seven or eight weeks because all the usual complications occur which is, drawing a strip which has Japanese characters but not being Japanese, people were worried about any racist insult they'd take from it...so, that was the first thing I did and it showed me it was actually possible to do something that you could tailor for a mass audience without actually having to compromise very much at all.

It was around about the same time you were doing a comic called Sinister Romance. This was during the Black and white boom.

WP: Yeah, it was. Back then any kind of black and white comic that was half way decent could sell thousands. So, Glenn Dakin and I decided we were going to do a romance comic, but it would be a stupid romance comic. We just did riffs on the typical romance situations. My favourite story was called 'The Words that Wound', about this couple who had problems because the bloke was always embarrassing his wife in social situations by saying outrageous things. So this whole, really conventional story was well written and quite funny in itself, where he finally promises after lots of embarrassing incidents, that he's going to stop upsetting his wife and take account of her feelings, be a more understanding husband and everything looks great, the two of them embrace and just when you think it's over, Aliens invade, robots come flying into the panel, and that's kind of how it ends. So that's the kind of thing I was attempting, because what's fascinating about storytelling is that you can always take something in a direction it shouldn't go in and thereby create some tension which can be resolved in some other way—it's one of my major preoccupations.

IC: SugarBuzz completists out there might like to know that two SugarBuzz characters in different forms make their debut in Sinister Romance: that's Mr Extra and Splash Girl. I don't know whether this is an influence of British comics, but I find the difference between what we do in SugarBuzz and what is American independent comics and some of these American cartoonists do is that we actually have a conclusive structure to the stories, there are definite endings and definite advancements. Whereas in a lot of American stuff you just kind of find there is no real conclusion, it's not really thought through.

WP: They get an idea, they play with it a bit and then they stop. And while that can be quite fulfilling for the artist, for the reader it's just frustrating because it doesn't lead you anywhere. And also because it doesn't require any real investment from the reader either. I like to create characters that relate to what people do and what people feel.

There's a lot of boring stuff in between... so let's skip to SugarBuzz and how it came to pass.

WP: Well I knew of Ian Carney a long time before I met him because for some reason I lettered a lot of things he had written.

IC: (laughs)And I was aware of Woodrow Phoenix because I'd read the Sumo Family. I was also aware of Ed Hillyer who shares a studio with Woodrow. For some reason and I don't know why because his name's not female, I was under the impression that Ed Hillyer was a girl. And I've absolutely no idea why, but I...

WP: Because he is a big girl.

It's the graffiti on the toilet wall. [laughter]

IC: At the UKCAC 1992! But, yeah, so it was inevitable that we were going to meet because, "Hey, the UK comic world's a very small place!"

WP: So, we happened to be staying at the same hotel as everyone was, at Glasgow, whichever year it was.

IC: We actually met on the Saturday afternoon and talked about 60's cartoons and Woods was talking about meeting Carmine Infantino...and we were talking about 60's Flash comics and weird Jimmy Olsen cross-dressing comics and all that kind of stuff. I think we discussed our common love of Frankenstein Jr and the Impossibles. We met next morning over breakfast with Garry Marshall who was drawing my strip Axis Mundi and there was actually a character called Bob...

Axis Mundi was the comic you did with Garry Marshall for Slave Labor.

IC: ...and Bob was a witty, sophisticated ape living in virtual reality who'd become like a God and wore a smoking jacket and smoked cigarettes and Woodrow professed a liking in that direction... [laughter] ...and I said I'd actually had the idea of doing a humour strip called Urbane Gorilla and Woodrow was immediately, "I'LL DRAW IT, I'LL DRAW IT!"

WP: Yeah. We discussed that whole phenomenon of urban guerillas. In the early 70's we used to hear on TV all the time about "Urban guerillas are running amok in the small town of ..."

IC: ..Wallasey...

WP: And I'd think "How can they talk about this so casually? Gorillas with guns are going berserk, and they're just skating over it on the news?!!" [laughter] "What's going on? Does no one understand what's going on in the world?!!"

IC: I remember phoning Woodrow while I was writing it and saying "Look, are we doing this as a straight Hanna–Barbera thing? 'Cos I'd kinda like to make it a bit twisted and slightly more dark..." and Woodrow said "Just see what suits the strip, go

The human body is our playground.

with what you want." And so instead of the typical Magilla Gorilla zoo and petshop that he escapes from it's a vivisectionist and characters got burned and stuff. Woodrow drew it and you know obviously it was great, it was the strip you see in SugarBuzz number one and in this collection. I mentioned that I'd quite like to do another one or something similar, and Woodrow said "Carry on!"

WP: Yeah because I really enjoyed doing it so much, because it had been quite a while since I'd worked with someone else. I'd been working with Chris Webster on Sonic [the hedgehog] the Comic, writing the Adventures of Ecco the Dolphin and he'd been drawing it and I'd drawn a couple of scripts that some other people wrote on some other Sonic stories and drawn the adventures of ToeJam and Earl from scripts by award–winning playwright Annie Caulfield. But it was really enjoyable to work with something that I could just create for myself rather than doing something that pre-existed and it was just fun because Ian and I really seemed to understand what each other wanted. I think originally we were going to send it to somewhere like Dark Horse Presents. But then it occured to both of us if we did lots more we could just do a comic.

IC: It was like "Hey, we've got a barn, we've got a band..."

WP: "Let's do the show right here!" [laughter]

IC: So, yeah, obviously Woodrow's worked with a lot of people, worked on his own, and I work with a lot of people. But I think when we actually work with other people that our styles are different, they're not like they are on SugarBuzz and I think when we come together to do SugarBuzz, it's like The Fly: Brundle/Fly—we're The Carney/Phoenix. Which is quite a pertinent analogy because like them we keep our penises in the Bathroom cabinet. [laughter] In the time after Randy the Skeleton which was so abstract, I wrote literally dozens and dozens of licensed titles, everything from Rugrats to Disney Afternoon and Power Rangers, Space Precinct, and the thing is there is absolutely no room for ambiguity in any of those strips: everything is very, very structured and even though SugarBuzz is completely ambiguous I think the actual structures are very, very tight, everything fits together.

You've had to throw away quite a lot of stuff, you have more material than you can possibly fit into the stories.

WP: There's not a wasted word or a wasted panel in SugarBuzz because a) we haven't got the luxury of the space to just throw things away and b) because we want to make it work, I mean, I like to make every thing earn its place so there isn't a superfluous comment or gesture because everything goes towards reinforcing the story one way or another.

It is a collaboration as opposed to someone writing a script and someone drawing it. How does that work?

WP: How it works is in every way you can think of. Sometimes Ian invents something completely and I'll just get a script, other times I invent it completely and Ian'll just finish it and then there's all the stuff in the middle where we talk about an idea for a while and then when we've got enough Ian'll go away and write it and then we'll fiddle around with it a little bit. It feels utterly effortless for Ian and me to come up with new things all the time. You know, we'll just talk about something and suddenly there it is, a story, and it's right there already without having to work very hard at it. It's partly because we've got to the point where we understand each other very well so we don't need to second guess each other and I trust implicitly that what Ian comes up with will interest me as well, so that whole kind of ego thing—who's going to control this thing—doesn't arise because what we're interested in is making it the best thing it can be.

IC: How we actually come up with most of the stuff is by basically just talking. I think, in terms of plots and what words are actually in the panel—that's what I do. The way the characters are formulated is always very different. I mean there's some stuff like Mister Extra or Splash Girl — I was looking at Sinister Romance and I thought well, they're great characters, I think they're worth doing, other stuff like Ultra Spacers Woodrow came up with the characters and designs and everything. Other times we've just come up with a funny name or concept and kicked it around. I remember Woodrow saying I want to do something with the line 'Ants in their pants' and we were just going "Mmm," I was saying I was thinking more along the lines of 'ants in the pant' or 'ant in the pants' and Woodrow said "Well, what about 'Pants Ant?' "

WP: And we both laughed so much for about five minutes and we thought "No it's too ridiculous, we can't," and then I thought "Wait a minute, we've got to do it! And that's why we've got to do it, because it's ridiculous!" One of the really liberating things about this is the way we're both really good at stopping each other chickening out, because a lot of the time I think what we're used to is never going as far as you really want to because you think "no one's going to get it, it's going to be too silly, too stupid," and what we did for each other over those first three or four issues was to constantly keep pushing each other, so I'd keep making Ian make it more stupid and he'd keep making me make it more ridiculous as well. So the ante kept being raised all the time. So now we're not afraid of being completely stupid because we know we can make it work.

What do you think you contribute individually to the strip?

WP: Well, obviously we have certain preoccupations which are contained within our characters...[laughter]

Like...? [laughter]

WP: ...Ambivalence. [laughter]
I think the nature of the human organism is ambivalence and that's where drama comes from.

IC: The human body is our playground. [laughter]
I think in terms of our personalities obviously we're quite different; to put it in Seinfeld terms, Woodrow's the Black hipster doofus and I'm the hyperactive White jerk.

Isn't it wonderful how comics can bring us all together like Stevie Wonder's keyboard?

WP: Yeah it is, we're all singing from the same hymn sheet.

IC: "Keyboard, pee–ahh–noh..." [laughter]
I think Woodrow comes from a more intellectual background and his approach to things...

WP: It's my curse, "My brain is my curse!"

IC: I think Woodrow is very analytical in a way that I suppose never having been to University, I feel I haven't got, um ...critical chops really. I think I react to something on a more instinctual level. Either I like things or I...DON'T.

WP: That them there things.

IC: That them there things. And I think Woodrow does kind of analyse. Is that true?

WP: Yeah, that's true.

IC: I think Woodrow always has a reason why he likes or dislikes something and...I...DON'T. [laughter] But, one thing... I need to say this — I actually think I have not got a very well developed Right hemisphere, but a...

WP: ...Superdeveloped...

IC: ...Superdeveloped Left hemisphere. And this is...when I'm thinking of ideas I actually walk around playing my bass and just like riffing ideas in my head and generally just play, play along to music or just play anything. But it was only recently that I thought actually playing guitar is a very right hemisphere thing to do: it's just further inhibiting the right hemisphere of my brain so that the left can go for a wander in the park.

So tell us about how your son became involved in SugarBuzz.

IC: Well, in many ways Jake's very like me, he's very up and hyper. He always comes up with loads of really great ideas and always makes loads of funny comments. I remember playing Batman with him when he was really young and I had the Batman toy and he had the Joker and he just suddenly shouted "Oh no, the Joker's stolen the President's magic telescope!" I was Just llke "Wow! Why can't more comics start like that?!" [laughter] When we were first doing SugarBuzz he was really interested in it because obviously it's cartoony and attractive to kids, so he was y'know "Oh, I really want to come up with an idea," and he came up with the idea of Future Crab. He had a Future Batman figure and he had this plastic crab and he was like "Oh no, it's Future Crab come from the future!" He came up with the idea of this character which we thought was great...

For some reason, it didn't occur to me for a moment that Valenteen was a gay character. He was just... "pretty."

WP: Ian and I were talking on the phone and he said "I was playing with Jake today and he came up with this great character called 'Future Crab,'" and I said "LET'S USE IT!!"

IC: But unfortunately for the first strip I didn't think of the idea of actually getting him to write it. So although he came up with the concept and some of the ideas, I had too much to do with that one unfortunately.

It wasn't pure.

IC: It wasn't pure. But after that, Dave Taylor asked me to do a one page strip for the United Kingdom Comic Art booklet and I mentioned to Jake about this and he said "Well, I'll do a Batman/Superman story." So we started from his 'president's magic telescope' story and he basically riffed on it for about two hours and I got down a one page strip from it which was absolutely abstract, but really funny and it was PURE Superman and Batman, it was almost primal Superman and Batman. And I thought "What am I doing interfering with the stories?" And then he came up with Dinosaurs versus Ninjas, which as we know is a classic, and we just went on from there.

But Jake's sort of pure ID.

WP: Yeah, Ian just interprets and writes down these words and then shapes them into a story and doesn't really have too much to do with them after that.

Tell us about some of his other characters, tell us the Midnight Moose story.

IC: He actually drew a picture of a moose on the blackboard in his bedroom in chalk and then in the middle of the night called us and said "Dad, Dad the moose on the Blackboard's really frightening me," and I said "Well, I'll just wipe it off," and he was just like "No! No you can't do that because the Moose'll be really angry!" So I was like "What can we do about it?" and we came up with the idea of actually drawing an 'on' and 'off' switch on the blackboard and putting it to 'off' which placated him. He tends to have a lot of these fevered, abstract notions.

What about the end of term art display at school, they'd been on a field trip to the beach...

IC: Yeah, the other kids had all drawn pictures of the beach seashells they'd found and all sorts of jellyfish and crabs and stuff like that and Jake had drawn this huge King Neptune impaling a shark on his trident with blood flowing out. And I was like "Mmm, I can't remember seeing that in New Brighton..."

What did his Teacher think of these things?

IC: Oh, she just thinks he's got a good imagination.

WP: That he has.

Also you have to get Jake hopped up on cheap orange squash don't you?

IC: We need to feed him Monster Munch and Golden Grahams.

WP: Plenty of yellow food colouring.

Where did Valenteen come from?

WP: Valenteen sprang fully formed from Ian's head actually and I just interpreted it. At first I was trying to figure out what kind of angle to put on him. I originally pictured him first in a gigolo kind of costume, sort of tight black pants and frilly shirts and big black hats. But Ian wanted something a bit more classically superhero–like so then we added the wings and gave him the pink costume and so on. Because, for some reason, it didn't even occur to me for a moment that he was a gay character, he was just somebody who was "pretty." [laughter]
But I soon found out what everybody thought...

IC: He's got a strong gay presence hasn't he? But actually the panel that everyone reacted to was the dog...

WP: Yes!

IC: ...sniffing the dog crap and then kissing Valenteen. [laughter]

WP: But that's what dogs do! [laughter]

IC: Yeah, everyone one was like "Ahh, it's disgusting!" but as Woodrow says, they do it all the time! I hate those people that kiss dogs.

But that's another of your motifs isn't it?

WP: It's kind of turned out that way — Animal kissing.

Animal kissing.

WP: But hey, if no one gets hurt I think what people do with animals is their own business—

Especially in cartoons. There seems to be a lot of emasculating imagery in SugarBuzz, **for example in** Pants Ant **with the Garden of Eden sequence.**

IC: Well one of my pet hates is pomposity, especially male pomposity and so any chance to de–bag—

WP: —Literally.

IC: Literally, I mean that was basically the whole 'Iron John' thing, which I find very hilarious.

WP: And of course implicit in the whole notion of what a superhero is there's always this kind of tension about what masculine identity is and it's always based around being very thrusting, virile, and words like that and the thing is most people are not 100% masculine or 100% feminine because human beings don't work that way.

IC: Woodrow's wearing a pink shirt as he talks. [laughter]

WP: Yes, it's true but that's because I'm very comfortable with my sexuality... [laughter] ..I'd like to point out!

...And a pair of matador pants!

WP: ...And a big black hat! [laughter]

WP: But, yeah, so most people aren't that and it's really amusing to play around with the premise that you can subvert—again—the notions of what heroines and heroes are and what normality is with just a very, very small adjustment which is all it is. It seems like a really huge thing to do because no one does it for some reason, but actually it's a very, very small thing.

IC: You see, Woodrow analyses that really well.

He does.

IC: "...Because I like to see men look silly!"

WP: See, he'll come up with the thing and I'll give you the theoretical framework for it.

Holiday Heroes?

WP: Well you came up with the idea for it ...

IC: Did I...?

WP: You came up with the idea of a group of heroes led by Father Christmas and we both thought that would be pretty hilarious.

IC: And I said I don't know what we can call it, it's got these kind of Holiday heroes and Woodrow goes "Uh...HOLIDAY HEROES?" [laughter] And I was going: "By Jove!!"

How did you get the individual characteristics of the characters? They're not how you would expect them to be.

IC: Well basically they're just, I mean, in some ways they're kinda like riffs on 60's superheroes, but I just thought the funny thing with Father Christmas would be him living at home with his Mum. I originally thought, the thing I originally suggested in the script was like...

WP: ...was a terraced house...

IC: Was a terraced house, but Woodrow said "No, it's got to be more gothic..."

WP: Well, because he spoke in that Thor/Shakespearean dialect it made more, it was funnier to me to put him in this grand setting behaving like he was living in a terraced house than to actually have him in a terraced house. Because again it's playing off those two expectations against one another.

IC: And I thought it was quite funny that his Mum was just feeding him products of her body. [laughter] ...But the other things like Halloweenie being the scaredy cat is basically just a play on the Barry Allen/Flash and the whole biological clock for the Easter Bunny was, well basically it came from the image of the egg which she used as a weapon and, and the Whitsun Table Lamp came from a particularly long session playing my guitar. [laughter]

So the next one was Splash Girl and Horse Eat Dog.

What happens between Major Nelson and Jeannie, in the bedroom? With all that magic ~~going around?~~

WP: Well Splash Girl was pretty straight forward; Ian remembered the Sinister Romance story which involved this character called Atlanta who had all the powers of the sea and we just thought she was a good character to have her own strip. Ian decided he would remix that story, so he changed her and made her...nuts. [laughter]
But it works, you know...

IC: And there's Horse eat Dog which is — I was having a conversation with some friends about the story of the song 'There was an old lady who swallowed a fly' and it was just obsessing me, saying "But like how many horses eat dogs?" and all this and I just thought "Horse eat dog? Yeah!"

WP: That's the least Woodrow of all the strips.

IC: Yeah it's funny, in some ways it's the least formal, formally structured.

It's the least based on any Hanna–Barbera precedent.

WP: Well a lot of them aren't really based on Hanna–Barbera. We just use them as a shorthand for talking about cartoons and that way of looking at the world that codifies everything into a nameable structure; and Hanna–Barbera itself doesn't actually feature that much in what we do—

IC: —Because we steal everything from Ruby–Spears. [laughter]
Remember what you were saying before about a lot of American strips just kind of ending in mid-story? That actually does. That does do that.

So you broke your own rule.

IC: Yes.

That's what they're there for.

WP: Exactly.

You Bad, Bad Monkeys?

WP: You Bad, Bad Monkeys was straight out of Ian's head; he said "I've got the script here, let's do it".

IC: I think it came from that childs' nursery rhyme which Jake, my son, was bouncing on the bed singing "No more naughty monkeys, bouncing on the bed," and I thought "yeah."

That's in the Holiday Heroes issue where there's another female character concerned about the ticking of her biological clock in that way.

WP: That was the Pregnancy Issue.

IC: Or the Non–pregnancy Issue. [laughter]

WP: Yeah, barren wombs...

You used the visual structure of an I Love Lucy comic.

WP: Yeah, I wanted that 50's kind of look.

My Wife—the Robot?

IC: Well that was after Woodrow mentioned that he liked drawing that 50's sitcom thing and I know that Woodrow really likes I Dream of Jeannie and Mr Ed and stuff like that, so I was just thinking "Well, what kind of disparate genre character type can I insert into this nuclear family...Domestic guy — Robot wife!"

WP: Of course. So again in order to make it as typical as possible I thought who is the best representative of that kind of idiom? I thought Jack Lemmon is the perfect kind of everyman so that's what that was. And that could be, that could go on for pages and pages and pages, but it's not really necessary because you know you get the joke fairly immediately.

IC: I think some lesser cartoonists would probably have spun it out to twenty pages.

WP: But we condensed it down to one page.

IC: Me and Woodrow were saying "What do you think, is this going to be a six issue mini series or a back cover?" [laughter]

WP: There are a couple more of those which we probably will do because it's just a great idea, we can't leave it alone with just one.

It's got one of the most disturbing endings of all your strips. [laughter]

WP: Well, because that's the thing implicit in those kind of stories. They never go as far as they ought to because of course the logical corollary of those kind of situations is that at some point the two characters' obvious lack of true meshing is going to come up...

IC: ...I know I was just waiting for that moment when Mr Ed kissed Wilbur and it just never happened. [laughter]

WP: Because you have to think to yourself what happens between Major Nelson and Jeannie, in the bedroom? With all that magic going around? So you know, no one ever talks about that!

IC: I think she had a beard underneath that veil. [laughter]

So there's a new strip in this collection as well.

IC: Yeah, Taking care of Lumbo and Lumbo who basically are just more annoying characters.

It's a Jim Carrey cartoon waiting to happen isn't it?

IC: Clancy Nothing Fancy, who's the everyman character, he's another pompous ... I mean in some ways he represents the everyman because he's the homeowner but he's also very pompous and obsessive and would be easily annoyed, especially by having two village idiots in his house. The idea actually came from, I was talking about Harvey Comics giants...

WP: Because all the characters in Harvey Comics are essentially super grotesque and really strange, if you actually thought rationally about them then you'd say "get out of my office!" to the person who came up with the idea because they're all nuts. But, no one questions them, BECAUSE THEY LOOK CUTE.

What do you think was going through the minds of those 1950's cartoon creators?

IC: Amyl Nitrate. [laughter]

WP: Martinis probably, Martinis and Long Island Iced Tea.

Because it was a super-straight society they were coming from and all their ideas were very, very strange.

IC: Well I honestly don't think that they were concious of the strangeness. I honestly think they were

just like sixty year old guys thinking "What are the kids into this week? We've got to do twenty Jimmy Olsen stories by the end of this month, twenty Superman stories by the end of this month — anything goes, guys!"

WP: I think one of the real strengths of approaching things with a very ordered, very superficially mundane, very structured style is that if they're presented right, the nuttiest things, you will just accept them because they're presented in a very reasonable fashion. And that's what I really like and I guess Ian as well about all those sixties Jimmy Olsen and Lois Lane comics, is that the stories are completely nuts, they are so mad, but they're drawn in this very, very, very straight forward, straight laced undramatic kind of style so you can just enjoy the lunacy without the self–conciousness of someone saying "Hey, look how mad this story is, hey look, look it's really crazy!"

IC: In some ways that is what SugarBuzz is, people will look at it and it's a traditional cartoony comic-looking comic with all these totally mad ideas and...

Do you think a lot of people actually miss that, if they don't actually read it they'll just look at it and ...

WP: Well the thing is that doesn't really matter to me because I know and Ian knows that there is nothing accidental in SugarBuzz, everything is there because we mean it to be there. And it's very satisfying to me to have that level of control and to know that I can put what I want into it. Obviously people get different things out of it and they get things out of it that you didn't expect and that just means it's working even better than you hoped because people start projecting their own stuff on to it.

IC: We had a letter about the proliferation of spirals in SugarBuzz representing a sign of madness and which I don't think we'd really consciously..

WP: But it's very true; in that issue of Pants Ant, spirals are everywhere as a little motif as the writer noticed: they're in the fingers of the crooks and on Pants Ant's trousers, they're in people's eyes and they're in backgrounds...

Humour will never get respect because hilarity undermines any rea- sonable debate.

Pants Ant seems to be one of the most success-ful of your characters; why do you think he is?

WP: Well lots of reasons really, but the prime rea-son is: Pants are funny.

IC: And the word 'pants' is one of the funniest in the English language.

WP: It is, it's got that plosive 'P' at the beginning, it's got the sibilant 'S' at the end, it's a very satisfy-ing word to say and pants are just rude.

Because in Britain it's a much ruder word than it is in the USA.

WP: That's true...well, I think it does have that con-text, that connotation, but it's not as strong as it is here.

Because it doesn't mean 'undershorts' as it does over here.

WP: Exactly. And it's just a great word to say, everyone likes saying the word 'pants'. We decided that 'Pants' and 'Ladies' were the two funniest words in the English language. 'Ladies' is also a very satisfying word to say.

IC: I was just talking to a friend and I mentioned that the two funniest words in the English language were 'pants' and 'ladies' so she said "so, presumably the expression 'ladypants' is the funniest expres-sion ever?" and I said "...yeah, it is!" [laughter]

WP: And fortunately we both laughed for a long time when the term 'ladypants' was coined, so that just shows how juvenile we are. [laughter] But yeah, because everything in Pants Ant's world is related to pants and we continually mention the word as many times as possible and use permutations of it as many times as possible, the whole thing becomes this self-reinforcing SPIRAL and it just gets sillier and sillier.

IC: And because it is so one note and we just kind of play that one note, it's a darn good note and we're going to play it 'til the cows come home.

It's like a humourous chinese water torture. SugarBuzz is a humour comic that's actually funny, why aren't all humour comics funny?

WP: Well, most of them are funny to somebody.

There aren't that many humour comics that make me laugh I have to say, but then that's partly because I've read a lot of humour things so it takes something special to make me laugh now or something unexpected or at least sure of itself. Most humour comics out there I find just far too ordinary. They don't take enough chances, they don't go far enough and they're not prepared to look silly. I don't respect any-body who's not prepared to look stupid for a good joke. I think good comedy has no sense of dignity, because dignity is not what humour's about.

IC: I think a lot of the problem with humourous writing, humour that's printed on the page, is that in order to appreciate the joke it has to be acted out in the reader's mind, and unfortunately people aren't that good actors. So the lamest line in something like Friends presented by a great comedic actor like Matt Leblanc can get a big laugh, but if you read that same line on the printed page it would be really flat. So, I think you have to sneak up on the reader and surprise them, because I think just laying out blank, predictable jokes just doesn't cut it. Woody Allen said that "Humour will never get respect because hilarity under-mines any reasonable debate" and that's true I think. I think in any medium really humour isn't appreciated enough. I mean it is an extreme reaction, and I think it's as valid a reaction as crying, in a film or a book or what-ever.

WP: There just seems to be something about the character of western civilisation that val-ues the serious, the weighty, the introspective, the apparently intellectual above the thought that a simple joke is valuable and I think it's very wrong, it's very wrongheaded but that seems to be the way people think. But I'm not here to challenge that notion, because I don't really care and it doesn't matter to me one way or the other.

IC: I think it's a lot easier to be superficially intellectual than it is to be funny.

I know I find it easier. [laughter]

IC: I think I may be building my own gallows here, but I do tend to think that if someone's really funny in comics they should be doing it somewhere else for loads more money. [laughter]
Maybe I'm just not funny enough to get out there, out of the comics ghetto, but hey, 'comics are my first love and they will be my last!'

Another thing I noticed about you, Carney, is that all great comedians are really depressed and you don't seem to be depressed ever. So, what does this say about you?

WP: There seems to be this notion that's been promulgated for a long time that if you are deep you have to be depressed...I think it's a lie to say that great comedians are always twisted and sad and messed-up people, because the ones that are like that are not very funny to me. You know, humour comes from a generous and happy and big hearted disposition. You can be critical and you can be mean-spirited, but that's not really funny y'know, it's sarcastic or it's cutting but it's not actually whole heartedly, good, genuine jokes is it? I mean when all the classic comedians started to get all jaded and pissed off, that's when they stopped being funny. I don't think you can really be funny unless you're prepared to whole heartedly accept your hidden frailties and just embrace them.
It's not cool to be happy, it never has been cool to be happy; it's cool to be depressed, it's cool to smoke cigarettes and wear dark glasses and talk about the futility of human existence. But actually it's very obvious that human existence is weird and futile, because the world is a very strange place and it's a very unknowable place and that's why we should tell jokes.

IC: A lot of great humour which actually shows itself in SugarBuzz involves seemingly superficial characters having great tragedy or perceiving themselves as having great tragedy in their lives.

There's a lot of resonance in SugarBuzz isn't there? It lingers after you've finished reading it.

WP: Well... that comes partly from my and Ian's belief I guess that any story that is interesting or good has to work on more than one level because everything in your life works on more than one level. Things are never that simple, there's always some-

thing else going on, there's always some underlying subtext, there's always another story and it's quite easy to get those kind of resonances going on if you are slightly more careful in the way you structure things; again it's that structure that gives you the ability to add layers and it's those layers that give characters just a little bit of depth.

IC: I think it's quite difficult to analyse what you do and it's very difficult to analyse humour because it ends up—

You just did it. [laughter]

IC: I know. We just did it.

WP: Yep, and it wasn't very funny.

IC: It's broken, we've broken it. [laughter]

So, do you think you're too busy trying to be clever?

WP: I don't see anything wrong with being clever, actually, as long as you're doing it for the right reasons. All I'm really interested in is making something as effective and interesting and as involving as it can be. And if that means I have to use my brain then that's okay.

IC: We just won't use it the issue after. [laughter]

Big Fat Girlie Kisses to:

Carole, Jake, Matt, Ed Ilya, Jake Steel, Geoff Coupland, Carl Flint, Andi Watson, Dave Taylor, Craig Pape, all the retailers who have supported SugarBuzz (you know who you are!), Brian Dixon and Cathedral, Jonathan Edwards and Louise, Evel Elson, Dave Robbo, the Hart–Davies Dynasty, Jackie and the Hot/Hit pack, Dick Hansom, P.G. Squires, Col Fawcett, Garry Marshall, Tish, Paul Gravett...

Pete Pavement, Anna Melting Vinyl, Nina Andrious, Craig Conlan, Lorna Miller + Chris, Erica Erica Erica Smith, Corinne Pearlman, Martin Butler, Mrs Bentley, Matthew Bookman, Howard Stangroom, Annie Caulfield, Frank Plowright, Chris Webster, Jean–Paul Jennequin, Christopher Longé, Nadia Sahmi, swinging Jay Grey, Philip The Boys, Martin Hand, Steven Martin...

Extra Big Fat Girlie Kiss to **Will Kane** (No tongue, though)

Ian Carney's Peccadillos include

Stella Artois, poor quality **KISS** bootlegs, Mike Maltese and Nicholson Baker, the Punky Meadows Shrine, Fountains of Wayne, Cafinesse, The Magic Whistle, Todd Rundgren re-masters, Metal Edge, the Royle Family and passive–Pokemon.

Woodrow Phoenix's Preoccupations tend to involve

Coca-Cola, Homicide: Life On The Street, 18th Dye, Meat, Robert Dranko and Phil De Guard in too many cartoons, Public Enemy, Ten–Pin Bowling, Tuxedos, Martinis, Frank Black, Chairs, Phil Silvers, NYC Board Of Ed Pencils, Ska, late nite shopping ...and **Catherine Landon.**